Where Saints Have Gone

poems

Wesley D. Sims

Iris Press Chapbook Series
Oak Ridge, Tennessee

Copyright 2025 by Wesley D. Sims

All rights reserved. No portion of this book may be reproduced in any form or by any means, including electronic storage and retrieval systems, without explicit, prior written permission of the author, except for brief passages excerpted for review and critical purposes.

ISBN: 978-1-60454-515-9

Cover Photo: Ken Lund

Author Photo: Brittany Cramer

Book Design: Robert B. Cumming, Jr.

Iris Publishing Group, Inc
www.irisbooks.com

Previous collections of poetry:

When Night Comes
Taste of Change
A Pocketful of Little Poems
A Funny Thing Happened on the Way to Maturity

To all those "saints" who attended
the little country "church in the wildwood"
beside the cemetery that inspired all these poems,
especially my relatives for five generations.

Contents

Cemetery ♦ 9
Silent Sanctuary ♦ 10
Gravestones ♦ 11
Huddling Histories ♦ 12
Saints ♦ 13
Ancestral Rivers ♦ 15
Last Words ♦ 16
Short Row ♦ 17
Two Beside Him ♦ 18
Scoundrel in the Cemetery ♦ 19
Resurrection ♦ 20
Corralling the Dead ♦ 21
Military Funeral ♦ 22
Lived Within His Means ♦ 23
Five Together ♦ 24
Return of Ashes ♦ 26
Angels ♦ 27
Stop Gloating Mr. Death ♦ 28
War No More ♦ 29
Little Ones ♦ 31
Two Memorable Dawns ♦ 32
One Unknown ♦ 34

Cemetery

Field of gray, granite
stones—inanimate monuments,

Engraved with departing dates
of those who touched our lives.
Inscribed with faded epitaphs

to console us, fill with hope.
Garden of enduring symbols,
reminders of the impermanence
of mortal life, the permanence
of relationships and memories.
Silent markers that remind us
who these now invisible people
once were and who we still are.

Silent Sanctuary

It seems a silent sanctuary,
quaint precinct of the dead,
wordless but sacred congregation,
a mausoleum of quiet bones
cocooned in metal or wood or dirt.
But strolling through it one
spring morning, I hear voices—
Father's laughter, Mother's advice,
Grandmother's prayer, Sister's
moan and death rattle.

As I browse among assorted
stone markers, shiny or pale,
some weathered and fading,
I can push buttons of memory,
replay words of many deceased
whose physical remains
reside here: parents,
grandparents, aunts, uncles,
neighbors and friends.

I can hear them speak once more,
familiar words I heard and stored
before their lives were stilled
by indifferent sentence of mortality,
their voices frozen in time,
sealed in shuttered recordings,
voices hushed forever
except in my recollection.

Gravestones

Assorted shapes,
they reach skyward
like small gray
launching pads
used by saints
for their spirits
to blast off,
overcome inertia,
gain momentum,
and accelerate
heavenward,
leaving the mortal
bonds of earth
in their envied
escape to eternal
weightless orbit.

Huddling Histories

The individual biographies
of these departed saints
sit scribed on scrolls of honor
in the upstairs records office.
But their histories and memories
huddle like teens at recess,
like football players
calling the next play.
They loiter in the cemetery
by their weathered tombstones
like off-duty angels
sitting on benches,
shrouded with pixie dust.

Reverend Jim is preaching,
Brother Irvin plays the piano,
Sister Lily leads the singing,
Grandmother is praying.
Mrs. Clark, and Barney,
and numerous others
just come and sit in the pews,
faithful stewards all.
Not for bragging rights
or competition do their stories
gather, they're just reminders
of kind and dedicated souls
that need to be remembered.

Saints

A congregation of witnesses paraded through this place,
people of ordinary status whose feet trod the way,
tainted with the soil of earth but whose heads sometimes
brushed the clouds. Servants whose minds believed
the Word, who felt the pain of others, with hands
that served neighbors who ached with grief and sorrow,
sickness and misfortune. They dished potato salad and grace.
Their souls reached for the eternal, their spirits
spoke compassion, embraced evangelism.

None of nobility nor royalty nor positions
of prestige, but tall trees who cast long shadows.
Some were friends or neighbors, some family.
Others' names and stories I heard about, many
from my mother, their faith, their perseverance.
They pushed always forward, like mighty rivers,
undaunted by boulders in their path. Holding on
to hope no matter the setbacks, enduring like stout
hickories, unbroken by storms that assailed and ravaged.

None became a Mother Theresa or Billy Graham
but like so many, they bloomed in the garden
where fortune planted them. Some wore Easter bonnets
and Sunday dresses but some donned cotton prints.
Some wore suits and ties, others jeans or work clothes.

Irvin played piano with nimble fingers. Lily led
the singing. Fagin always offered handshakes.
Gracie, a prayer warrior, decorated with peony bouquets.
Louise practiced the admonition *Let the little ones
come unto me.* Reverend Jim preached forty years.
Some with fabulous voices rang the rafters with solos.
Barney warmed the hickory-hard benches
every week. Nell taught Sunday School a long time.
Countless others held various positions and offices.

Those spirits who departed here, seemed to ascend
from the launch complex of this small country church
and cemetery. Rose upward like chimney smoke
on a crisp autumn morning. I imagine they
hesitated, hovered a brief moment as if to bid
farewell to us earth-bound pilgrims
left behind to finish our race. They left
their weary bones to bless the community,
and to remind their heirs of service. They left us
meditating on lives well-lived, on churchmen
who earned the salutation, *Well done thy good
and faithful servant.*

Ancestral Rivers

Memories of the dead hover
like spirits over the beloved
cemetery where two rivers
of ancestors merged and spawned
tributaries branching into
ever more living streams.
Each generation spread like forks
of a giant, multilayered oak tree
whose long, winged shadows
from many outstretched limbs
fell across the astral plane
of this honored place, blessing
the land, hallowing this garden
of vining connections.

Last Words

Jim and Sally rest
in eternal silence now,
their weathered bones
comforted in consoling sod.
No epitaph on their stones.

Never talked much.
No children to evoke
a storm of dialogue.

Depression era folks,
practiced in frugality,
used words like a precious
commodity. Perhaps they took
to heart my great-grandfather's
admonition, "Some things
are better felt than said."

Jim's last love words:
I tried to do right by you,
always ate the end piece
of bread so you wouldn't
have to.

She offered the final
benevolent psalm,
over his corpse,
like a true stoic,
I loved the end piece
but saved it for you.

Short Row

In the middle
of a country
cemetery,
too easy
to overlook,
only children.
Short row,
short stones,
short lives,
a short time
for memories.
Brief, bright
butterflies,
they gifted
us their
unique beauty.
Now flown
up there,
a long, long
time of joy
brightening
the halls
of heaven.

Two Beside Him

They likely knew each other
but how could they know
they would both be companions
and worthy wives to this same
honorable husband? And
both lie down beside him
for their eternal rest.

The first died too young.
Too many children,
too much wartime weariness,
too much pain and illness.
A still healthy man with a farm
needed another wife, and
the second woman needed him.

Now his marker stands book-ended
by their white tombstones.
Silent testaments to human
needs, to pragmatism, to love
and peace. An amiable trio
resting now in the currents
of the endless river of time.

Scoundrel in the Cemetery

Someone sneaked a scoundrel
into the graveyard
of dearly departed saints,
tearing a dark hole
in the hovering holy mist
like a crater bruising the ground
from a rotten apple falling
off the tree of knowledge.

Resurrection

The skirt of lush green grass
trimmed, he scrubs with vinegar
solution the dust and stains
from every letter carved in granite.
Washes and polishes her monument
as though it's her new house,
until it gleams in slant of evening sun
like the angel brooch she often wore.
Places a bouquet of robe-white roses,
kneels in front of the shiny marker,
back bent with crippling grief
heavy as a wooden beam.

Touches the emblazoned cross emblem.
Runs his fingers over the cuts
of epitaph as though reading Braille,
his eyes blurred by streaming tears.
He begs again her forgiveness
for the wrongs that strained
their relationship at times,
for salt sprinkled in open wounds.
And for his sins of omission—
the many times he denied a warm
embrace, an unrestrained kiss,
a heartfelt *I'm sorry*.

How often he missed looking
into pleading eyes, declaring
with heartfelt emotion, *I love you*.
Now he pours passion
into too-late words and misplaced works
as if a tidy gravesite and contrite heart
might call forth a resurrection.

Corralling the Dead

I recall as a child
the family cemetery beside
the little wooden church,
bordered by a metal fence,
strong posts and sturdy iron gate
as though to corral dead citizens
like horses lest they wander off
when nobody watched the herd.
The fence meandered along the road,
looped down by woods' edge
and back around by the church.
Was it meant to keep out the living
or hold in the dead?

Older and wiser I learned
it could not do either.
We went in to visit family plots
as necessary, to clean or decorate
graves or just to refresh our minds
with facts—when did great-grandpa
die? How old was uncle John?
What was my infant nephew's name?

Cloistered, bloodless bones couldn't
rise and walk. Spirits of the dead
promptly soared heavenward.
But memory-ghosts of many I knew
drifted out and around their stones.
Some danced through the webbed
wall of wire whenever
I strolled nearby with eyes to see.

Military Funeral

His mother sits beside the open grave
an American flag drapes the coffin.
Her first son's military funeral held
without a body, one of the first
killed in Pearl Harbor attack.
This one lived past sixty, but now
he is receiving final honors.
The seven-member honor guard
stands fifty yards away, white gloves
holding their rifles in the air,
their faces stern as the bare
gray trees this cold December day.
The bugler, white as an angel, plays *Taps*,
seven guns fire a salute,
smoke puffs hover like frosty breath.
His mother's face is solemn
but drained of tears.
Two sailors in dress whites
perform their ritual, salute
the Stars and Stripes,
slowly fold and hand it to her.
The funeral director lowers
the casket, pays his respects.
She and family and friends
slowly move away as the assistants
start tossing shovels of dirt.
Hugs and quiet conversations begin.
A mother should not have to
bury her children.

Lived Within His Means

She lobbied for granite double stone
with vase for flowers, but thrifty Tom,
long married to meagerness,
insisted no extravagance.

She stuck him on a small plot,
back corner of country graveyard.
His marker made of two
weathered boards, one held
name and dates hand-painted,
the other with small yellow
letters scribbled on black
proclaimed his motto—
He liked to live within his means.

Five Together

The tall marble monument stands
in stately beauty, but its weathered
gray and white exterior blurs
the dimmed inscriptions
of names and dates as though
it is ashamed of their truths,
as though it can't bear
to reveal their grim statistics.

Forty-year-old mother's name
in front, two daughters on one side,
two young sons on the other.
One son died at seven,
the other when one year old.
Daughters left at four and five.
Three children and their mother
all deceased within ten months,
in late 1899 and 1900.

Was it measles or smallpox,
consumption or tuberculosis?
Did a lamp burn all the anxious
hours too many restless nights,
a fevered child cradled in trembling arms?
How many bleary mornings
could she not pull her aching body
from the bed when dawn's relentless
light pierced her windows?

Did hot springs boil when hell
itself bubbled up in the backyard
loosing the pale horseman—
   Coming for your children?
Walls bleeding at last
with futile screams of the mother—

When will You be satisfied?
Did heartache push her body
to the grave, spent and hopeless?

Their bones lie nestled now
together, forever in one grave.
Their stories unpublished,
mind-numbing details
speak enough—four unlucky
children and mother in her prime
stolen away too soon.
Events that cause even believers
to whisper, *Where is God?*

Return of Ashes

Fifty-odd years he moved among us—
   breathing, feeling, thinking,
strong of frame and will,
   fulfilling his unique destiny.
Traveled to many places around the world.
Became a soldier, served his country,
   defending freedom. A nighttime
plane crash cut short his busy life.

Transported in a small plastic vial,
   distillation of mortality reduced
to inanimate essence, his ashes
   prepared to return to the earth.
These gray elements once joined
   in organic compounds, vibrating,
pulsing with the mystery of life.

His energy transmitted
from the eternal source,
   passed to him like fire
   that the Cherokees transferred
campfire to campfire
from the original source,
   its flame never allowed to die.
   Until the mysterious call
that extinguished a singular flame,
the one whose allotted time expired.

His remains were placed
   on his grandmother's grave,
left to season and seep,
   mingle with her residual elements.
A rejoining of dust with dust
   where we can remember
their cherished and departed spirits.

Angels

On a walk in the churchyard
late on a humid summer afternoon,
swift dark clouds recede eastward,
give way to brightening sky.
Small white pillars drift near
and swing low, reminding me
of Great-grandfather's visitation.
While he strolled here
one burdened evening an angel
descended and hovered nearby.
Lost to me in ancestors' passing down
the story, the purpose of his emissary's visit.

Was it a guardian angel
offering protection and assurance?
Or an enforcer of a name change
like the one who wrestled Jacob?
Or an escort come like a sung-about
chariot to shuttle away a saint's spirit?
I like to imagine a messenger angel
come with the often tendered gift
of assurance, *Fear not.*

Stop Gloating, Mr. Death

So you took down a healthy victim
yesterday, robust, bright-eyed hero.
Cut short another cheerful song.
Thought you had one more today,
but we sprang an interception,
shut you out this time.

I've seen your work—most weak
specimens you've gathered, too weary
from months or years of illness,
too lacking in energy and hope
to mount a challenge. I know
your technique—come sneaking in,
a thief in darkness, riding
your pale horse, scouting easy prey.

But wipe that devilish smirk.
Your day will come. Maybe
you're so busy searching your directory,
nailing new pinups on your victory wall—
bruised, pallid faces you've selected—
that you haven't yet heard
of the physical law of entropy.
How, left to its own resources,
everything winds down in due course.
And the other, higher law—how there's
an appointed time for everything under the sun.

Enjoy the bountiful gleaning in your season.
But look in the mirror tomorrow morning,
inspect your hair, look close for streaks
fading to gray, framing wrinkled skin.

War No More

Five Civil War veterans buried in one
small cemetery in Leoma, Tennessee,
among my ancestors. Repressed memories,
brutal nightmares laid to rest.

John remembered—the fatigue of bodies
marching days and nights like battalions
of ants, going days without food,
sleeping on the cold ground in rain and snow.

Timothy tried to forget—the roar of canon,
incessant booms of musket attacks,
staccato thud of bullets, tearing down
wave after wave of blue and gray soldiers.

Hank still nursed nightmares—
screaming soldiers, limbs blasted off,
mini-ball wounds, amputations,
creeping infection, slow painful deaths.

James could never erase some scenes—
squalid wallows, disease and exposure,
indescribable hunger and hopelessness
in the Andersonville, Georgia POW camp.

Robert fought to keep his sanity in the war—
worried about family back home
coping with shortages, fear and desperation,
their last milk cow confiscated by soldiers.

The survivors spoke no more
of atrocities, suffering and sacrifices.
No more of politics, fear and anger.
But they couldn't kill their memories.

Free now to "study war no more,"
their bones repose in undisturbed peace,
their permanent discharge granted,
their battlefields morphed to a silent mural of sky.

Little Ones

> *Let the little children
> come unto me… of such
> is the kingdom.*
> —Mark 10: 14 KJV

In the late 1800's
and early 1900's
many came—infants,
toddlers, youngsters.
With smallpox
or measles,
consumption
or tuberculosis,
various maladies
or accidents.
Plucked up
like lily stems
for bouquets.
Nurtured, mourned
and grieved,
blessed and buried,
precious rose buds
planted and watered
with copious tears
to blossom in heaven
as stunning flowers,
decorations to line
the golden streets.

Two Memorable Dawns

The sun beams strong this morning
glinting on the dove-white marble
tombstone of my great-great-grandfather,
my centerpiece of the cemetery.
Two wives buried on either side of him,
the first worn down by sacrifice,
war-time burdens, and deaths
of three young children.

I cannot fathom the trouble he tasted.
Endured deep darkness of the Civil War
living in Alabama woods
to avoid conscription and killing,
and to help feed his family.
Like the veterans of that war,
he didn't talk about those lean years,
those mean and trying years—
living on wild game and hard tack,
avoiding rattlesnakes and soldiers,
seldom seeing his children.

Near war's end he brought his family
to Tennessee for a fresh start,
a place to forget lost family members.
A quiet man, gentle soul, conscientious
objector, his eyes held deep compassion
and the blue of a summer sky.

Perhaps it was the war,
or the loss of his children
and father to measles and small pox.
Or maybe the voice he heard
near a rose bush ablaze with healing
sunshine one desperate dawn
after losing his only son,
that shook his soul and warmed his heart.

He claimed the promise, kept his vow,
became a Methodist minister.
To share good news and offer hope.
To teach others how to embrace love
and transform swords into plows.

One Unknown

No name or information posted.
Only an old brown field stone marks it.
We don't know if the person entombed here
in this small cemetery was male or female.
Other unmarked sites exist here,
so I will assign this one female.
Might have been a distant cousin or aunt.

Age and status unknown.
Parents and heritage unknown.
Was she old or young, a small child?
Death caused by smallpox, pneumonia, childbirth?
Was she rocked by a heart-broken
parent or did she rock a child in her last days?
She could have been a wife.
Maybe a beloved mother.
Did someone cry at her death?

Who shared her dreams and fears
that vanished in this patch of country soil?
Any descendants or relatives forgot her,
never came to place a tombstone
or any marker with name and dates.
Why was her grave abandoned
by everyone who knew her?
I planted a single rose by her stone,
retrieved from my grandmother's bouquet.

Not a nameless ghost.
Should not be another Jane Doe.
She was some mother's darling.
Maybe a father's pride and joy.
Born a member of the human race,
she had worth, deserved remembrance.
She was a child of our Creator
and He who knows when a sparrow falls
must have grieved her passing.

Acknowledgments

Thanks to the editors of following publications in which the following poems first appeared in some form.

Breath & Shadow: "Two Memorable Dawns"
BloodRoot Anthology: "Scoundrel in the Cemetery"
Quill & Parchment: "Last Words," "Lived Within His Means," "Short Row"
Poetry Pod: "One Unknown"
Poetry Quarterly: "Five Together"
Magnets and Ladders: "Ancestral Rivers," "Cemetery," "Gravestones," "Silent Sanctuary," "Huddling Histories," "Return of Ashes," "Stop Gloating Mr. Death," "Two Beside Him," "Angels"
Slate & Style: "Military Funeral"
Songs of Eretz: "Resurrection"
Voices on the Wind: "War No More"
Word Gathering: "Corralling the Dead"

Wesley D. Sims has published four chapbooks of poetry: *When Night Comes, Taste of Change, A Pocketful of Little Poems,* and *A Funny Thing Happened on the Way to Maturity.* His work has appeared in *Artemis Journal, Bewildering Stories, Breath & Shadow, Connecticut Review, G.W. Review, Liquid Imagination, Novelty Magazine, Pine Mountain Sand and Gravel, Plum Tree Tavern, Poem, Poetry Quarterly, Proverse, Quill & Parchment, Songs of Eretz, The American Diversity Report, The South Carolina Review, Time of Singing, Word Gathering,* and several other journals and anthologies. He has had poems nominated for Best of the Net and the Pushcart Prize.

www.ingramcontent.com/pod-product-compliance
Lightning Source LLC
Chambersburg PA
CBHW021002090426
42736CB00010B/1423